# How Big Is It?

## A Book about Adjectives

by Cari Meister
illustrated by Holli Conger

amicus readers

3

# Say Hello to Amicus Readers.

You'll find our helpful dog, Amicus, chasing a ball—to let you know the reading level of a book.

## 1

### Learn to Read
High frequency words and close photo-text matches introduce familiar topics and provide support for brand new readers.

## 2

### Read Independently
Some repetition is mixed with varied sentence structures and a select amount of new vocabulary words are introduced with text and photo support.

## 3

### Read to Know More
Interesting facts and engaging art and photos give fluent readers fun books both for reading practice and to learn about new topics.

Amicus Readers are published by Amicus
P.O. Box 1329, Mankato, MN 56002
www.amicuspublishing.us

Illustrations by Holli Conger
Editor Wendy Dieker
Designer Heather Dreisbach

Printed in the United States of America.

10 9 8 7 6 5 4 3 2 1

Library of Congress Cataloging-in-Publication Data
Names: Meister, Cari, author. | Conger, Holli, illustrator.
Title: How big is it? : a book about adjectives / by Cari Meister ; illustrated by Holli Conger.
Description: Mankato, Minnesota : Amicus, [2017] | Series: Say What? Parts of Speech |
Identifiers: LCCN 2015041500 (print) | LCCN 2015046773 (ebook) | ISBN 9781607539308 (library binding) | ISBN 9781681510545 (eBook)
Subjects: LCSH: English language--Adjective--Juvenile literature. | English language--Parts of speech--Juvenile literature.
Classification: LCC PE1241 .M44 2017 (print) | LCC PE1241 (ebook) | DDC 428.2/4--dc23
LC record available at http://lccn.loc.gov/2015041500

An adjective is a word that describes a noun. A noun is a person, place, or thing. The **purple** words in the story are adjectives.

Scarlett, Arjun, and William are hiking. The three friends are in the park.

"Wait!" says Scarlett.
"I see something."

"What does it look like?" asks Arjun.

"It is big and hairy and brown,"
 says Scarlett.

"Let's follow it!" says Arjun.

"Maybe we should go home instead,"
 says William.

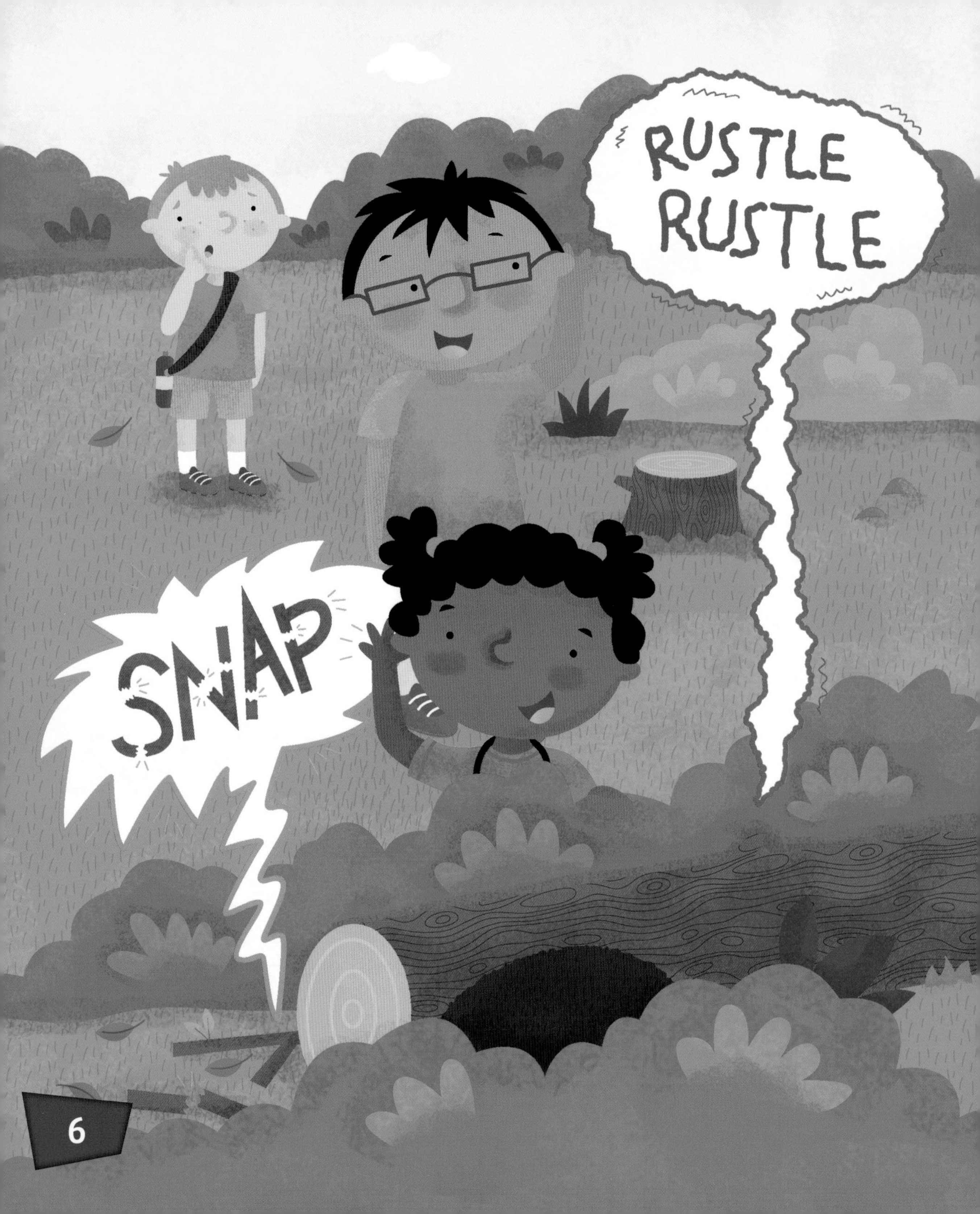
RUSTLE
RUSTLE
SNAP

"Shh!" says Scarlett. "I hear something."

"What do you hear?" asks Arjun.

"I hear a snapping sound," says Scarlett.

"I hear a rustling sound," says Arjun.

"Let's get out of this creepy place," says William.

"There it is!" says Scarlett.
"The animal is going to the pond!
I see a tail."

"What does the tail look like?"
asks Arjun.

"It is thick and flat," says Scarlett.

"Oh good!" says William.
"That means it is not a grizzly bear.
Grizzly bears have stumpy,
fluffy tails."

Scarlett laughs.
"No, it is not a grizzly bear!
It is not that big."

"You said it was **big**," says William.

"It *is* **big**," says Scarlett.
"It is **bigger** than **a** squirrel
or chipmunk."

"Look," says Arjun.
"The big, hairy, brown animal
with the thick, flat tail is a beaver!"

# Jobs of an Adjective

Adjectives can describe a noun:

**Grizzly bears have stumpy, fluffy tails.**

**A, an,** and **the** are adjectives. They tell us which noun:

**The animal is going to the pond!**

Adjectives can describe how many nouns:

**The three friends are in the park.**

Adjectives can compare nouns:

**It is bigger than a squirrel or chipmunk.**

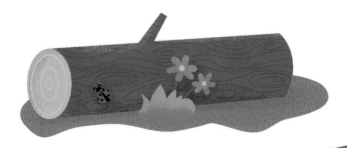